Original title:
The Pocket's Wisdom

Copyright © 2025 Creative Arts Management OÜ
All rights reserved.

Author: Sophia Kingsley
ISBN HARDBACK: 978-1-80586-223-9
ISBN PAPERBACK: 978-1-80586-695-4

The Archive of Age-Old Thoughts

Inside the corners, stories hide,
Where lost socks and gumdrops bide.
Old receipts and lint conspire,
To weave a tale that won't expire.

Each crumpled note, a past delight,
A coupon for a frozen night.
The wisdom of a mustard stain,
Is worth its weight in laughs and grain.

Joys Pressed Against Fabric

In crinkled threads, a treasure trove,
A button that makes the cat feel bold.
Faded tags with prices ripe,
Whisper secrets of the hype.

There's candy wrappers, full of cheer,
And napkins with our thoughts austere.
A stash of jokes, they hide from view,
These little laughs we've picked right through.

The Assurance of Felted Memories

Wooly things that bring a grin,
A relic from the time we've been.
Knitted hats from winters past,
Whisper memories built to last.

Each thread a laugh, a tickled seam,
Stitched with laughter, woven dream.
A pet's old toy and crumbs of bread,
In felted layers, joy's not dead.

Little Secrets of the Stitch

Behind each seam, a giggle grows,
With playful tales that nobody knows.
A zipper's fumble, a button's drought,
These silly moments we can't live without.

Patchwork stories, a colorful mix,
Where laughter's the thread and joy's the fix.
So pull up a chair and peek inside,
These little secrets we can't abide.

Hidden Gems Beneath the Flap

In the depths of my jeans, a world is alive,
Coins dance in the dark, they take quite a dive.
Chewing gum memories, stuck like a charm,
Lost little treasures come out to disarm.

The lint's a magician, it makes things disappear,
A sock from last winter has finally shown here.
Bobby pins mingle with wrappers askew,
In this merry mayhem, what fun will ensue?

Tucked Away and Treasured

A button lost ages, I find it once more,
It laughs at my fashion, a style I ignore.
Old receipts chatter, they share stories grand,
Tales of what I bought with a wave of the hand.

A stray earbud lies, it dreams of good tunes,
Imagining concerts under bright, swirling moons.
A treasure map drawn in pockets so deep,
Guides me to snacks that I promise to keep.

A Journey in Shrunken Spaces

What a tour through a pocket, a capsule of time,
Where candy wrappers jive, and coins play a rhyme.
A twist of a gum wrapper, a slip of a note,
Adventure awaits where imagination floats.

A tiny world bustling, a kingdom amassed,
Where old shopping lists live, as legends from the past.
The crumbs are like royalty, crumbs of delight,
Banishing hunger, oh what a sweet sight!

Curiosities in Cotton's Embrace

A keychain's secret, puzzled and wedged,
Hiding from prying eyes, quite unpledged.
A mystery button, its story untold,
In the seams of existence, oh hot and so bold!

The lost marshmallow, a snack of great lore,
It's sitting quite snug, I'm sure there's a score.
In the fabric's delight, surprises abound,
Making me giggle with treasures I've found.

The Voice of Unseen Impressions

In my pants I keep a stash,
Of lint and crumbs, a hidden cache.
Each piece a story, tiny, neat,
Of meals, mishaps, and messy treats.

A gum wrapper from a scene so sweet,
Wrapped up laughter, can't be beat.
A rogue coin whispers tales of woe,
Of vending machine dreams gone slow.

A forgotten receipt adds to the lore,
Of that shirt I bought, I still adore.
These bits of life, tangled and bold,
Unlock the joy in stories old.

So dig deep down in your old jeans,
Find wisdom in crumbs, not just routines.
The unseen lives where chaos blends,
In every pocket, laughter transcends.

A Journey in the Fold

Within my pocket, secrets dwell,
A crumpled map, an uncharted spell.
Each wrinkle tells a tale profound,
Of mishaps lost, yet laughter found.

A lucky charm, a rubber band,
Both hitchhiked here, not quite planned.
They've shared my ride, through thick and thin,
In every fold, there's fun within.

Old batteries whisper of power spent,
While tiny receipts are well-content.
They hold the economy of my spree,
A journey spent surprisingly free.

So fortune's joy, in pockets lies,
Amidst the junk, the small surprise.
Each treasure found, a playful note,
That life is wild, in every coat.

The Art of Hidden Insights

A paperclip, bent, now a key,
Unlocks the laughter, just for me.
In odd corners, wisdom waits,
Beneath the weight of grocery fates.

Old napkins crumpled, a fortune told,
In ketchup stains and doodles bold.
They sketch a story, of meals shared,
In every scribble, love declared.

A scrap of fabric from last night's dance,
Whispers of fun, the unplanned chance.
These small artifacts, a merry crew,
Reveal the laughter, shining through.

So dive right in, explore the mess,
Each hidden gem can surely bless.
Forget the fuss of formal insights,
Embrace the giggles, life's delights.

Leftover Threads of Experience

In pockets deep, the stories fade,
Of socks mismatched and crumbs well laid.
Each thread a moment, stitched with fun,
In this fabric of life, we've just begun.

A button lost, a tale it keeps,
From clothes so wild, their history leaps.
They tell of parties and moonlit nights,
Where laughter echoed, raising sights.

A sugar packet, sweet and sly,
Hints at coffee, late-night pie.
It's a sugar rush and giggles shared,
Amidst the chaos, love ensnared.

So poke around at what you own,
Find joy in threads, no need for moan.
The lessons learned, in fabrics free,
Find wisdom here, as we all agree.

Tucked Away Truths

In my coat, a treasure trove,
Lint and crumbs from snacks I strove,
A forgotten note, a love so sweet,
And half a sandwich, my midday treat.

A key to nowhere, lost some time,
A rubber band that stretched in rhyme,
Old train tickets, tales to tell,
All tucked away in my pocket's shell.

A straw for drinks, a penny too,
Each little thing has its own view,
A crumpled receipt, math gone wrong,
Yet here they gather, a merry throng.

When life gets grim, I take a peek,
And laugh at memories, quite unique,
For in this fabric, life unfolds,
With hidden stories, bright and bold.

Depths of a Stitch

In the seams, oh what a sight,
Fabric swirls like a kite in flight,
A button's missing, but who will care?
I've found a sock, it's quite the pair!

A needle, waiting, glad to hear,
Stories whispered in cozy cheer,
A thread of fun, a splash of hue,
In every stitch, a joke to view.

Pockets deep with secrets spun,
Like a magician's escalating fun,
A patch of laughter, a dash of glee,
Hidden wonders, just for me.

So dare to peer beneath the fold,
And find the quirks that life has told,
In every stitch, embrace the play,
Where laughter lingers, come what may.

Memories in the Lining

Beneath the fabric, tales reside,
From every adventure, they cannot hide,
A gum wrapper, sticky and bright,
Recalls the day we took our flight.

A forgotten ticket for a show,
With laughter spilling, a night aglow,
And crumbs from cookies, sweet and fine,
All snuggled close in the garment's line.

A small toy car, wheels still lost,
Takes me back to childhood's frosty frost,
Each little item, a chuckle heaps,
In the lining, where silliness sleeps.

To rummage through is pure delight,
Finding joy wrapped up so tight,
In pockets' depths, the past can shine,
With giggles echoing in the twine.

A Glimpse of the Unseen

A paperclip, bent just a tad,
Holds memories of times I had,
With scribbled notes that make no sense,
Yet in my heart, they build the fence.

Lost keys jingle, a playful tease,
They hide away, as if to please,
In chaos, laughter blooms so bright,
A glimpse of joy, out of sight.

A ticket stub from long ago,
A night of fun, a sparkling glow,
With crumbs of popcorn, laughter shared,
In secret pockets, dreams are bared.

So dig within, it's worth the search,
Where silly moments gently perch,
A treasure chest, unseen but near,
With every find, a reason to cheer.

Threads that Bind Us

In a pocket small, secrets hide,
Like socks unmatched, they bide their time.
Old receipts whisper tales untold,
Of groceries bought and treasures sold.

A crumpled note with doodles bright,
Messages in pencil, a comic sight.
Lint and laughter dance in there,
A curious world, beyond compare.

A button loose, a story shared,
Of nights in haste when no one cared.
Each trinket saved, a friendship's thread,
With every laugh, our worries shed.

So rummage deep with a chuckle loud,
In mystery cloth, let joy abound.
For in this space, both wild and free,
We find the bonds that laugh with glee.

Wisdom Lightly Worn

An old receipt, it tells no lies,
Of takeout nights and donut fries.
With wisdom gained from every bite,
A lesson learned, from taste that's right.

A thumbtack glints, a tale to share,
Of workplace pranks and wild affair.
Sticky notes in colors bright,
Words of wisdom, light as light.

A hairpin's bend, a laugh, a sigh,
A secret kept, who knows why?
Every scrap holds history fun,
Adventures lived, under the sun.

So cherish all, this pocket's haul,
From serious dreams to lunchroom brawl.
A tapestry of whim and grace,
With laughter stitched in every space.

Secrets Wrapped in Fabric

Beneath the lint, a story brews,
Of missing socks and coffee views.
A scrap of cloth, a colorful thread,
Holds laughter soft, where fears are shed.

A forgotten candy, sweet and old,
An epic quest from days of gold.
Each wrinkle holds a giggle bright,
In every fold, there's pure delight.

An errant key, a puzzle's piece,
Unlocks the fun, allows release.
Each hidden gem, a silent cheer,
In pockets deep, adventure near.

So dive into this fabric's fold,
Where secrets dance, and dreams unfold.
With every treasure we might find,
We laugh, we play, and unwind.

Traces of Tales Untold

A napkin scribbled, ideas fly,
Of wishes made, beneath the sky.
A paper airplane, once took flight,
Now folded up, but dreams ignite.

Stickers stuck to corners tight,
Bear witness to our playful plight.
In every corner, stories blend,
In that small space, we transcend.

A shoelace tangled, like our plans,
Yet laughter springs from awkward stands.
With every trinket, joy unspools,
In pockets deep, we craft our rules.

So cherish all these snippets small,
For in these threads, we find it all.
With humorous hearts and pockets wide,
We uncover life's splendid ride.

Where Lessons Linger

In folds of fabric, secrets hide,
A sock with tales, an egg surprise.
The lint offers tips, if you abide,
Check twice before you claim the prize.

A crumpled note, a penny's kiss,
They whisper gently, share a laugh.
Old wrappers dance in joyful bliss,
Saying, 'Life's too short for a stiff giraffe!'

Each pocket holds a curious tale,
Of mismatched socks and crumbs galore.
So take a peek, set your sights,
You might find wisdom, or just a chore.

So if your pockets feel a bit tight,
Just stand up tall and dance with the light.
For riches come from funny things,
Like rubber bands and magical springs.

Glimmers of Knowledge

Dig deep in fabric, you'll find the zest,
A set of keys and an old test.
The gum that lost its sticky quest,
Teaches us all to find the best.

A bag of jellybeans, bright and bold,
Offers flavors, if truth be told.
Lessons wrapped in wrappers gold,
In each sweet bite, let wonder unfold!

Change jingles cheerfully within,
A silver coin with tales to spin.
From shiny thoughts to proud chagrin,
Life's simple truths can make you grin.

So shake your pockets, give a cheer,
Learn from laughter, toss out fear.
For what you find in cloth and seam,
Might just inspire the wildest dream.

The Path of the Tapestry

Adventure waits in each thread and seam,
A ticket stub for the late night dream.
A napkin note, a secret theme,
Unraveling laughter, a silly meme.

In the pocket's depths, a treasure's glow,
A rubber duck, a rubber snow.
It quacks with joy, don't you know?
Life's tapered edges—let your worries go!

Whimsy swirls in every nook,
Pockets' stories—just take a look.
From forgotten coins to a fairy book,
Magic awaits in every crook.

So pull out giggles, don't you fret,
From fabric's folds, there's no regret.
For in this tapestry we weave,
Laughter's treasure's what we believe.

The Hidden Alphabet of Experience

In corners of pockets, secrets reside,
A crumpled receipt, the stories inside.
A gum wrapper whispers, 'Remember that day?'
Life's little lessons, tucked neatly away.

A lint ball's a scholar, wise not quite grand,
Teaching us patience, like grains of sand.
A forgotten ticket, a trip gone astray,
Shows us the fun in getting lost, hey!

An old button chuckles, it's seen quite a show,
While coins jingle joyfully, 'Come join the flow!'
Each small bit of clutter, a tale on its own,
Bringing laughter and wisdom, wherever you've grown.

So next time you reach for a tissue or snack,
Remember the treasures that cling to your pack.
In pockets so humble, life lessons unfold,
With a giggle and grin, let their stories be told.

A Tale in the Tuck

In my coat's secret pocket, a mystery waits,
A loose paperclip, and a few paperweights.
A sprinkle of dust, and a fluff from a sock,
Curious treasures, all snug in their flock.

A cranky old marble, with stories to share,
Claims it once played games, with monkeys in air.
A piece of old candy, now rock hard and bold,
Claims 'I'm still sweet, just been waiting to mold!'

Each pocket a portal, to laughter and fun,
With bits of adventure, one by one.
A lone mint with dreams, of being a treat,
And tales of a journey, beneath your seat.

So dive into pockets, let the fun unfold,
With trinkets and treasures, each story retold.
In laughter we find, what's silly and grand,
A world tucked away, at the touch of your hand.

The Remarkable in the Ordinary

An old pen in my pocket, forgotten but spry,
Jots down a joke, in the blink of an eye.
A rubber band stretches, with stories to spin,
Of summer days gone, and the fun that's within.

A crinkled napkin, it holds a great plan,
For an epic quest, with a sneaky old man.
A bottle cap hints at a drink once enjoyed,
Memories bubbling, never fully destroyed.

A stray button grumbles, 'I used to be chic!'
Now I hang on, just a little antique.
Yet all these bits, so humble and meek,
Add laughter and color, to the things that we seek.

So look to the ordinary, give it a glance,
For in simple pleasures, we find our romance.
Each item a verse, of life's playful tune,
In pockets we gather, the joy of the June.

Memories Etched in Cloth

A frayed edge of denim, a tale from the past,
Of a wild summer dance, and the joy they amassed.
The threadbare patches wear stories of cheer,
Of laughter and mishaps, that linger so near.

A faded old handkerchief, soft like a sigh,
Wipes tears of laughter, while waiting to dry.
A stitched up corner whispers secrets of style,
Reminders of moments, that make life worthwhile.

In pockets of fabric, where memories dwell,
Each snag and each seam casts its own magic spell.
A silly ol' sock, with one lonely twin,
Is proof of adventures, and where we've been.

So cherish those textiles, let fabric ensue,
For each little stitch holds a laugh or a view.
In clothes we find wisdom, and stories to weave,
As life rolls along, let's just laugh and believe.

Everyday Insights

In the depths of my coat, I find,
A crumpled receipt, secrets entwined.
It showed I bought snacks and a drink,
A treasure in fabric, don't you think?

A forgotten coin, shiny and bright,
It sparkles like stars in the middle of night.
It teaches me joy comes in small things,
Like laughter that dances and happily sings.

Lost keys jingle with tales of their fate,
Unlocking the moments, aren't they great?
They wave their goodbyes when I'm in a rush,
But lead me to adventures, oh what a hush!

So here's to my pocket, my clever friend,
With wisdom that bends, it never will end.
In the chaos of life, it helps me collide,
With laughter and lessons I keep by my side.

Pause and Reflect in the Fold

I reached in my pocket, oh what a find,
Gum wrappers and lint, a treasure combined.
Each piece a reminder, a giggle, a hey!
Life's little chaos, so fun in a way.

Change jingles softly, like reminders of fun,
A penny for thoughts, amongst the run.
In every small crevice, a giggle to seek,
Whispers of joy, of laughter, and cheek.

A crinkled old note, perhaps a love line,
Scribbled in haste, but oh how it shines.
It brings back the giggles from long days ago,
A sweet little memory—the pocket's own show!

So pause for a moment, dive deep in the cloth,
Find the bits of life that warm and that froth.
There's wisdom in small things, so quirky and bold,
Life's laughter and magic, lovingly told.

Patterns of Resilience

A button gone missing, a thread hanging low,
In the fray of the fabric, new lessons can grow.
Each snag and each tear tells tales of the bumpy,
Yet laughter persists, even when grumpy.

A tissue half crumpled, a friend from the past,
It caught all the giggles that faded so fast.
It whispers of moments both silly and sweet,
Reminding that life can be light on its feet.

Candy wrappers dance like confetti of dreams,
Each rustle and crunch a testament it seems.
To the sideshow of life, both wacky and wise,
Patterns emerging, just look in your eyes.

With each little finding, resilience does bloom,
In pockets of fabric, there's always more room.
So throw in your worries, your laughter, your glee,
Life's playful enchantments—come look and see!

Remnants of Reflection

In the fabric of time, I find bits of cheer,
A forgotten old note that brings a small tear.
It's signed with a doodle, a smile, oh so wide,
Reflecting the moments that we try to hide.

A hairpin that whispers of styles long ago,
Where fashion was fierce, and trends would bestow.
It giggles at fads that came, went, then stayed,
Remnants of days that were wild and unfrayed.

A mint from a friend, the flavor of laughs,
In pockets of joy, our memory drafts.
Each morsel and trinket, a story does hold,
Remnants of friendship that never grow old.

So delve in your pocket, don't let it collect dust,
It's a vault of good times, in memories we trust.
For laughter and love are just a reach away,
In the remnants of life that brighten our day.

Echoes of Forgotten Moments

In the depths of my old coat,
Lies a crumb from last year's toast.
A mystery of ancient meals,
My taste buds dance with silent squeals.

A ticket for a movie long gone,
Faded dreams on a Sunday morn.
I laugh at the ghosts of popcorn fights,
As I search for change in dim twilight.

What secrets hide in this fabric maze?
A lone sock recalls its better days.
A pen that once wrote love's sweet note,
Now rests in peace—a paperboat.

Each item a tale, each crumple a jest,
A peek inside brings a hearty quest.
I chuckle at what my pockets conceal,
In a world of puns, they spin and reel.

Threads of Insight

Buried deep in my favorite jeans,
A mint wrapper and some old routines.
A toothpick from a steakhouse feast,\nOffers wisdom, at least a yeast.

With every item, a chuckle grows,
Like time travelers in goofy clothes.
Missing keys from a lock once fit,
What a saga, a perfect skit!

I find a fortune from last week's gum,
A trio of wishes, all quite dumb.
One request? More snacks, but how to fit,
In a pocket already full of wit?

A button perhaps, from a shirt once bright,
Whispers secrets of laundry night.
Each small treasure in fabric defined,
Holds laughter's spark, forever entwined.

Whispers in the Fold

At the seam of my well-worn bag,
Lies an old receipt—a grocery drag.
It tells of veggies and pastions had,
But only of snacks it's making me glad.

A rubber band stretched thin with glee,
Just a notion of playful decree.
It snaps at air like a puppy's chase,
In my pocket, there's a quaint little space.

A forgotten mint from the cinema's fray,
And a fortune cookie's crumpled say.
"Good things come to those who wait,"
Or just to those who have snacks on their plate.

Each whisper echoes of life once lived,
A stash of laughs where joy is sieved.
In the folds of these fabric-spun dreams,
Laughter bubbles, or so it seems.

The Keeper of Small Things

I'm the keeper of what once was grand,
A napkin doodle, a paper band.
In each crease, a chuckle resides,
With lost toys and candy confides.

A mysterious coin from who knows where,
It jingles softly, a melodic flair.
A treasure map sketched in a child's hand,
Leading to snacks in a make-believe land.

A pebble that sparkled like no other,
And a sticker featuring a smiling mother.
These moments tucked, they wiggle and sway,
In every pocket, a humorous array.

So here's to the small, the silly, the bold,
Treasures of laughter, forever retold.
With each wandering thought that life might bring,
Embrace the joy that small things can sing.

Unveiling the Ordinary

In a world of pockets wide,
Change and crumbs love to hide.
Keys that jingle, lost in cheer,
A mystery woven out of beer.

Socks that vanish, there they go,
With popcorn kernels in a row.
A gum wrapper tells a tale,
Of a weekend that went pale.

How did that banana peel arrive?
Did it roll from a kitchen dive?
Life's secrets tucked, it's quite absurd,
In a place like this, who's ever heard?

A penny here, a ticket there,
Each one leads to a lost affair.
Laughing at the junk we keep,
In these folds, the wonders creep.

The Weight of the Unsaid

Shhh! What's hidden in this space?
Unspoken truths, an odd embrace.
A gumdrop, a note, who can say?
Each silence whispers, 'Take me away!'

Old receipts, reminders of blame,
Like the time I misplayed a game.
Change that rattles, stories in flight,
Old loves lingers, just out of sight.

Burdens resting, thoughts that cling,
Like the sweater I meant to bring.
In this fabric, tales obscure,
A giggle hides, yet feels so pure.

Weightless worries, soft and slight,
In pockets where the lost take flight.
Embrace the clutter, join the dance,
Life's a circus; give it a chance!

Curiosities Among the Threads

What wonders lurk in seams so deep?
A rubber band that cannot leap.
A crumpled note, a map of sorts,
Plans of adventures and wild sports.

Bobby pins and other odd mates,
Holding together life's debates.
Lint that dreams of a higher cause,
Ticklish tales amid the flaws.

The button lost, the clothing wars,
A condiment from last night's scores.
From hitchhiking days to shopping spree,
These treasures speak, just wait and see.

Each thread a banquet served with glee,
In pockets small, a grand decree.
With chuckles shared and treasures found,
Life's quirky charms astound, abound.

Layers of Unexpected Truths

Beneath the fluff, what lies awake?
A cheeseball grin from a birthday cake.
A fortune cookie, cracked in fun,
With wisdom that won't be outdone.

Forget-me-nots and instant ties,
Connections formed by crafty spies.
A straw hat worn for lazy days,
Amid the chaos, laughter stays.

Tangled threads, ties that bind tight,
Beneath the mess, a joyful sight.
A DIY kit, half-assembled fears,
Yet here we sway and toast with beers.

In layers thick, absurd and bright,
Every pocket tells its plight.
So let's divulge what we abscond,
In laughter's arms, we find the bond.

Abiding Stories in Hidden Corners

In the cuff of my jeans, a treasure I find,
A gum wrapper crinkled, a story entwined.
It whispers of candy, of flavors so bold,
And laughter of children, those secrets of old.

An old shopping list, with a scribble or two,
Seems to mock my attempts at a diet anew.
Yet, each item listed invokes a big grin,
As I dream of the feasts that I planned to begin.

Fuzzy lint balls dance, they conspire and scheme,
Mismatched socks giggle in a whimsical dream.
They plot for their freedom, a grand sock parade,
While I search for their mates that I can't seem to aid.

So here in my pockets, small tales intertwine,
In the fabric of life, where the comical shine.
From crumbs of my lunches to notes from my friends,
The laughter's in waiting, the joy never ends.

Little Lessons in Threaded Tales

A button once lost, yields wisdom profound,
For every loose string, there's a lesson unbound.
With fabric soft stories stitched tight with a throng,
A patch for a tear, where we all still belong.

Lurking in seams, a fortune cookie's fate,
Promises of fortune that make up for late.
Each crisp little snippet, a chuckle or two,
Life's quirks and oddities, just waiting for you.

An old receipt winks from the dark of my jean,
With snacks and some laughs, 'twas a riotous scene.
It tells of adventures, the bites shared in glee,
And moments when buying just felt wild and free.

So here in my pockets, oddities sing,
Like coins with their stories, oh, the joy they bring!
For woven in fabric are laughs yet untold,
Just waiting to surface, like treasures of gold.

Mysteries Held Close

Beneath the old lint, a legend resides,
Of a sock's great escape, where mischief abides.
It vanished one morning, slipped out in a flash,
Leaving only its mate for a curious clash.

A broken crayon, stuck deep in the seams,
Bears witness to colors of childhood dreams.
With swirls of bright laughter, it whispers and beams,
Of doodles and giggles, adventures and schemes.

The crinkles of papers, a note left behind,
In scribbles and doodles, my past unconfined.
"Oh, promise to keep me," it begs with a grin,
To stay tucked away where the fun can begin.

So delve in the pockets, uncover the laughs,
In the mysteries held where mundane meets half.
In the stories we stash, our joy starts to shine,
For even the smallest can sparkle divine.

The Weight of Small Things

A pebble I pocketed, claimed as my prize,
Weighing down my jeans, but worth every size.
It glimmers like laughter, a reminder I keep,
Of times I was adventurous, dreams in a heap.

Half a mint left, now an old friend of mine,
Its flavor still whispers, "Go ahead, take your time."
A hint of past sweetness, with giggles and glee,
An ode to the moments that hang on a spree.

Scraps of old napkins, heart-felt doodles show,
A sketch of a kitty with a cheerful hello.
Each line tells a story, a giggle to find,
There's wisdom in laughter; it's brilliantly kind.

Embrace the small treasures that hang in your pants,
Declare that each item deserves its own dance.
For the weight of small things can lighten the day,
With humor and charm in the silliest way.

The Geometry of Life's Fabric

In the folds of fabric, we all find,
A triangle of laughter, so unconfined.
Life measures in circles and quirky lines,
Patchwork designs of our silly minds.

Stitching our stories with threadbare wit,
A square of mischief where humor sits.
Angles of chaos in orderly rows,
Patterned by moments that nobody knows.

When life seems a rhombus, do not despair,
Just draw a few doodles, hang loose in the air.
Triads of giggles, pentagons prance,
Geometry thrives in our clumsy dance.

So let's weave together this tapestry bright,
With stitches of joy that dance through the night.
For in this grand fabric, we all have a part,
Crafting a quilt from the heart to the heart.

Sown Reflections

In the garden of thoughts, seeds drop like rain,
We plant quirky notions, yet harvest the plain.
A funny patchwork of dreams intertwined,
With weeds of confusion and laughter aligned.

Reflecting on moments that sprout unexpected,
We giggle at shadows, so easily flecked.
Each sprig holds a story, a chuckle, a grin,
Growing wisdom from folly, where does it begin?

The sun shines on creases of silly concerns,
Where growth has a rhythm, and laughter returns.
With petals of humor, we shape all we see,
Tending these blossoms so joyfully free.

So plant all your worries in soil that's absurd,
Let them bloom brightly, absurdly, unheard.
For in every reflection, a lesson will sprout,
With giggles and whispers, we'll laugh it all out.

The Strength in Smallness

In pockets of treasures, small finds gleam bright,
A button, a jingle, a key, pure delight.
Tiny adventures in every little space,
Compact little stories, each one filled with grace.

A crumb left behind tells a tale of a feast,
Of laughter and chaos, happiness released.
Small joys in a minute, a wink, and a grin,
The little things whisper, let the fun begin.

In corners so tiny, we gather great strength,
A whisper of humor that spans every length.
For fortune is often in things that we wear,
A speck of pure joy we willingly share.

So cherish the wee bits, embrace their great worth,
In the tiny small wonders, we find our mirth.
For life's greatest riches are often concealed,
In moments, not grand, but simply revealed.

Collage of Moments

A snapshot of giggles, a clip of delight,
Stuck to the canvas, all scattered in sight.
Memories colorful, like paint gone awry,
Each brush stroke a chuckle, a wink in the eye.

From fragments of laughter, we craft our display,
With glue made of joy, we stick them each day.
Cut-outs of chaos, glued down with a grin,
In this collage of moments, our fun will begin.

Snapshots of silliness, tossed in the air,
A polka dot memory, quirky and rare.
With scissors that snip at the mundane and meek,
We trim the ordinary, the gentle and sleek.

Each slice tells a story, each hue hides a joke,
In layers of humor, we'll dance and evoke.
For in this grand collage, a life we create,
Is stitched with a smile, it's never too late.

Whispers from Worn Fabric

In the depths where crumbs reside,
Small secrets from snacks collide.
Buttons giggle, threads entwine,
A hidden world, quite divine.

Lint rolls laughs from pockets deep,
Where lost change starts to creep.
Old receipts tell tales of woe,
Of things we bought, that now won't go.

Sticky gum with stories stuck,
A sliver of luck, or just bad luck?
Tissues rustle, bear their weight,
Of sneezes past, and dinner dates.

Yet through it all, a charm still thrives,
In every fold, a life survives.
So dive right in, embrace the jest,
For wisdom's in the mess, I guess!

Secrets Sewn in Stitches

In seams where mysteries can bloom,
Hidden treasures find their room.
A thread of red with stories spun,
Of clumsy dances and laughter run.

A pencil case sings of dreams,
While crayons plot in colorful schemes.
Each rip a moment, each patch a tale,
Like gossipy friends at a lively trail.

Worn-out fabric throws a grin,
For every tear, there's adventure in.
That old sock whispers loud and clear,
'Life's too short, just grab a beer!'

So wander through, let stitches guide,
Where quirks and giggles coincide.
In every fold and every crease,
Laughter dwells, and worries cease.

Echoes of Forgotten Charms

Beneath the flaps of pockets old,
Whispers of journeys yet untold.
A paperclip, bent with grace,
Hints of mischief in this place.

Lost keys laugh from their hiding spot,
What doors they'd open—oh, why not?
Receipts crinkle with stories slight,
Judging the snacks eaten at night.

Old gum wrappers do a jig,
A disco ball, it's quite the gig!
Every fold, a dream's embrace,
Echoes dance, surreal and base.

So tip your hat and strike a pose,
For wisdom hides where no one knows.
With colorful depths, explore with glee,
In forgotten charms, life's tapestry.

Lessons from the Depths Within

In corners dark, where dust bunnies play,
A rogue button rolls, in wild dismay.
Coins clatter with a cheeky cheer,
'Buy yourself something nice, my dear!'

A receipt chuckles, crumpled and grim,
Highlighting meals that felt quite slim.
The elegance of a threadbare seam,
Holds the stories of every dream.

So grasp the oddities, hold them tight,
For laughter's found in the most unlikely sight.
Lessons gleaned from pocket's nest,
Show life's a jest, and we're all but guests.

So dive inside, don't be afraid,
Every scrap has a joke to be made.
From linings deep, let friendship spin,
The laughter echoing from within.

Time's Soft Whisper

In a world where secrets hide,
A sock can guide you, take a ride.
It holds more than just a fluff,
With tales of lost keys, it's enough.

A button's tale of love gone stale,
With threads that tell a silly tale.
Did it really hold a dress so grand?
Or just a napkin, stained by hand?

A coin might jingle, loud and clear,
Reminding us of the last time here.
Each wrinkle tells a laugh or tear,
In pockets deep, our dreams appear.

So when you dig, just take a chance,
Find treasures there that make you dance.
Embrace the quirks, let laughter flow,
For wisdom hides in pockets' glow.

Recollections in Tightly Woven Fabric

In the seams of laughter, secrets dwell,
A ripped old shirt tells a tale so swell.
The fabric whispers, soft and light,
Of pizza stains that brought delight.

An old belt holds a stubborn grin,
As it tightens up with a little spin.
Once a fashion icon, now a twist,
Who knew it would be such a tryst?

Tangled yarn shows a cat's delight,
Playing hide and seek in the night.
Every knot holds a little cheer,
And a warning for whom we hold dear.

So cherish the threads with every find,
The cozy mess, the quirks that bind.
For in this fabric, we learn and play,
With funny memories brightening the day.

Beyond the Simple Stitch

A stitch may seem just perfectly neat,
Yet often it hides a hidden feat.
What's that lump? A candy surprise,
Left from the last laughter-filled pies.

A needle tucked won't prick your grin,
Though it might just hold some cheeky sin.
Behind the seams of what we wear,
Are stories tangled everywhere.

A patch of bright, an odd patch too,
What journey did this fabric brew?
Each thread a tale of joy or woe,
With laughter stitched, it starts to show.

So don't ignore what threads unfold,
For simple stitches may be bold.
They carry laughter through every sway,
In quirky patterns, life's ballet.

Tapestry of Life's Lessons

A tapestry woven with giggles and sighs,
Holds memories bright as the sun in the skies.
Each thread a lesson, each knot a joke,
Beneath it all, the silly smoke.

An apron that caught a flying pie,
With pockets stuffed, no reason to cry.
A badge of honor, a chef's delight,
In kitchen battles, a whimsical fight.

The colors clash and sometimes fade,
Yet every patch is a memory made.
Dance with the spools, twirl with the loom,
In laughter's embrace, life finds its room.

So weave your fabric, fun and bright,
In the weave of day, find pure delight.
For in this lesson, we see the cheer,
In a tapestry's heart, humor is near.

Treasures of Tattered Edges

A crumpled bill with stories told,
Laughed at by coins, a sight to behold.
A cigarette butt has wisdom to share,
And gum stuck to soles, unaware of despair.

Old receipts with dreams left unspent,
Tell tales of dinners and money well lent.
A lint-filled treasure, a sock's missing mate,
Sits proudly in pockets, refusing to wait.

A ticket stub from a movie long past,
Whispers of laughter and friendships meant to last.
Loose change that jingles, a chorus of cheer,
In the depths of our pockets, life's goofballs appear.

So dive into fabrics, embrace every rip,
Unearth hidden gems on this comical trip.
For in every corner, however askew,
Lies a giggle, a chuckle, each day something new.

The Unfolding Narrative

A crinkled map of adventures gone by,
Guides us to wonders, oh me, oh my!
A scribbled note that says, "Don't forget!"
Leads to old snacks that we can't regret.

The story unfolds with every unfold,
A mix of surprises and marvelous gold.
Old gum wrappers tell of summer's delight,
While napkins narrate a mishap one night.

Stray buttons remind us of outfits that failed,
Each pocket a chapter where laughter prevailed.
A hairpin once lost, now a relic of lore,
Unlocks all the times that we danced on the floor.

In these fibers of fabric so snug and so neat,
Lies a history only our laughs can repeat.
So cherish your pockets and all they unearth,
For in their small worlds, there's infinite mirth.

Intimate Imprints

The pocket is cozy, a vault of our mess,
Where crumbs take a toll and socks join the stress.
A sticky note whispers, "Call me tonight,"
Reminding us gently to keep love in sight.

A stray hairpin, a fragment of fun,
Holds secrets of laughter from bright days begun.
Pocket lint tales of a journey once vast,
Connecting adventures both future and past.

Lost marbles roll deep in the folds,
Reminders of childhood when life was pure gold.
A gum-chewed wrapper tells of sweet treats,
As mishaps ensue with each laugh that repeats.

In these soft spaces, so special, so true,
Lie memories stitched with a giggle or two.
So dive into pockets, let whimsy reside,
In intimate imprints, our joy is our guide.

Small Wonders in a Stitch

In seams and folds, small wonders abound,
Bright threads of laughter in pockets are found.
A paperclip soldier, a brave little troop,
Marches alongside a lone chocolate droop.

A tiny key, where does it belong?
Unlocks all the stories we danced to in song.
The dandelion fluff from a day in the sun,
Whispers of wishes and countless times fun.

Bits of old fabric, a quilt of delight,
Wraps us in memories that spark joy at night.
Lost earrings giggle at the things left unsaid,
While happiness dances where each seam is thread.

So gather these wonders, don't let them flee,
For in every pocket, there's magic to see.
A stitch of pure humor, a weave of sweet bliss,
In the fun of small finds, how could we miss?

Enigmas of Everyday Carry

In my bag, a snack that sings,
A rubber band with high hopes swings.
Keys hum tunes of places far,
While old receipts tell tales bizarre.

A stray pen that hardly writes,
Yet claims to be an artist's sights.
Mints expired, a mystery bold,
Planned for freshness, truth be told.

Lost my phone, it's gone astray,
But I've got a rock and some play.
Marbles rolling think they're wise,
Filling pockets, oh what a prize!

My wallet giggles, full of dreams,
Jokes it whispers in paper seams.
Crumpled coins in a dance of cheer,
Every carry holds a secret near.

Treasures at Hand's Reach

In my pocket, a treasure map,
To locate snacks, a quick recap.
Chewing gum with stories to tell,
Yeah, it's stale, but folks can't tell!

A crumpled note that claims I've won,
But I lost track of the fun.
A button missing from my coat,
Who knew it had such a vote?

Old glasses that no longer focus,
Seeing everything, that's hocus pocus!
A paperclip that thinks it's grand,
Holding together more than planned.

Balloons deflated, a party's ghost,
Yet in my pocket, I love them most.
Every find, a joyous scream,
Pocket treasures, a silly dream!

Hidden Lessons Within

Lurking deep in my old coat,
A lesson learned from a spilled oat.
Stains and crumbs, oh what a ride,
Pockets tell of where I bide.

A tiny charm that lost its shine,
Reminds me laughter's truly fine.
Leftover receipts, a math debate,
Spent too much on pie, it's fate!

A mystery sock, where did it go?
Partners once, now a solo show.
Bits of lint with whispers deep,
Pocket wisdom, secrets keep.

I find old coins from long ago,
Each one's a tale, a gleeful show.
Life's odd lessons tucked away,
A funny thought to start my day!

Secrets Sewn in Fabric

In my old jacket, secrets fold,
At the seams, tales left untold.
A lint ball spins a yarn or two,
While thread debates the hue it knew.

A missing button sings a lark,
It's lost its way in the dark.
The zipper giggles, can't zip it tight,
As my keys jingle with delight.

My pockets hold each clumsy spill,
A chocolate bar that gave me a thrill.
Wrappers dance like confetti bright,
As I recount my snack-filled night.

Fabric whispers, laughter and cheer,
In every fold, the fun is clear.
Each little secret makes me grin,
Cloth with charisma, let the fun begin!

The Unfolding of Small Wonders

In shadows of fabric, a secret resides,
A crumb from a sandwich, where mischief confides.
Coins jangle like laughter, a melody sweet,
In pockets of chaos, life's odd little treats.

A receipt from last month, a tale of a spree,
A tiny lost toy, just as happy as can be.
Old gum under quarters, now stuck to the seams,
A treasure map hiding in old faded dreams.

Socks that no longer match make a curious pair,
Whispers of adventures, that linger in air.
Each fold holds a story, new giggles to share,
The hidden delights of a pocket's own flair.

With each playful rummage comes joyment and glee,
Every nook and cranny, a world we can see.
So dive into those treasures, let laughter flow free,
In tiny conclusions, life's mysteries be!

Harvesting Insights from Cloth

A t-shirt from high school, with stains that still glow,
Yells of past parties, where did all that cheer go?
Loose change spills the secrets, of days gone awry,
While crumpled up notes carry hopes to the sky.

The lint is a sage, wizened from wear,
Shucked from old sweaters, with stories to share.
A forgotten old receipt, still holds its own flair,
Counting every whimsy, like gems from a fair.

With socks that conspired to dance on their own,
And crumbs from a cookie, sweet laughter has grown.
Each pocket a party, where stories ignite,
Harvesting chaos, to create pure delight.

So lend your hand deep; savor what's found,
In pockets of fabric, there's wisdom abound.
Sift through the laughter, let giggles entwine,
Finding joy in the scraps, like sun in the brine!

Secrets Beneath the Surface

Beneath the old fabric, mischief awaits,
Sticky gum and lost keys whisper sweet fates.
A pen that once traveled, now idle and stale,
In pockets of mystery, there's always a tale.

Fuzzy receipts map out a journey untold,
Chasing down tales, as laughter unfolds.
A lone rubber band, quite the daring rogue,
Unraveling stories from where they once stowed.

Feathers and buttons, the ghosts of a fling,
Echoes of laughter, where strange treasures cling.
With each deep dive, a surprise waits for you,
In secrets that hide, like a good joke that's new.

So dig a bit deeper, embrace the absurd,
Treasures of nonsense, in silence, unheard.
Glimpse all those whims that keep bubbling near,
And chuckle along with each delightful cheer!

Flutters of Inspiration Within

Within this old jacket, a dance of delight,
A crumpled up napkin, with doodles so bright.
Random receipts boast of fast-food glories,
Each slip holds a laugh and remarkable stories.

A tiny soft monster, lost once in the fray,
Now guards all the giggles from every old day.
Sweet cookie crumbs gather like friends in a jest,
In this whimsical chaos, we've all been so blessed.

An elastic band, worn but full of great charm,
Keeps secrets together, with a pocketful's arm.
The laughter of moments, captured in seams,
Each flutter of fabric, ignites silly dreams.

So rummage for joy; let adventure begin,
For pockets hold treasures, both wild and within.
Unlock all the laughter that lives on each thread,
And find inspiration in what's easy, not dread!

The Unwritten Ledger

In the depths of my jeans, oh what a find,
A mint from last summer, I must be blind!
A crumpled receipt, a half-eaten snack,
The wonders that dwell in my pocket's backpack.

Change jingles like laughter, a comical tune,
Pocket treasures dance, under the light of the moon.
Each coin tells a story, each note a delight,
My pocket's a ledger, rolling through the night.

Forgotten gum wrappers from days long lost,
A pencil, a keychain, what's that, a frost?
Life's little humor in each tiny nook,
In my pocket's wild world, I find the best book.

So, here's to the treasures, both silly and sweet,
My unwritten stories, make my day complete!
They pile up like wisdom, soft as a feather,
Oh, the joy of a pocket, light as a tether.

Keepsakes of the Everyday

What a strange hoard lives inside my jeans,
A lonely button, a few old routines.
An expired coupon, a bit of fluff,
Packed with life's essence, though sometimes it's tough.

I reach in for keys, but find jellybeans,
A bizarre collection from sight unseen.
With each flip and tug, laughter ensues,
The pocket's a keeper of whimsical views.

A paperclip army, ready to march,
They thrum with excitement—oh how they arch!
A tattered old napkin with doodles galore,
It writes me a tale, I can't help but adore.

In the vault of my pockets, I treasure the small,
Each quirky artifact stands proud, not at all.
So here's to the junk, and the giggles they bring,
In keepsakes of life, I hear the heart sing.

Hidden Gems in the Seam

In the seam of my pocket, a mystery lies,
A candy wrapper, where flavor never dies.
A single lost sock from an epic game,
Why must my pocket always be to blame?

Treasure hunts thrive in this denim-filled sea,
A scribbled note sings, 'Don't forget to be me!'
Old tickets for films, like ghosts of the past,
Which superhero won? The suspense holds fast.

With cringe-worthy finds, I can't help but smile,
A fortune cookie slip—that's been here a while!
A forgotten crayon, it dreams of the page,
Waiting for colors to stoke its old rage.

Hidden in seams, comedy reigns,
Lost in a jungle of mundane chains.
In the pockets of life, let laughter commence,
Unearthing the gems, it's simply immense!

Notes from Beneath the Surface

Beneath the surface, hiccups and cheer,
A grocery list dances, 'Get milk'—oh dear!
Crumbled up dreams wrapped in a joke,
Each fold a reminder, or perhaps it's just smoke.

A lost marble rolls, in search of the crew,
Did it fall from a child? Who knows? Not a clue.
Among coins and lint, secrets proliferate,
My pocket's a circus—come join and relate!

Sticky notes whisper of genius undone,
They laugh while they wait for the battle to run.
An old sunglasses tag, and yet, no shades found,
Just a pocketful of joy, mixed with life's sound.

So reach in and plunder with gleeful intent,
What lies in your pocket? An adventure well-spent!
Notes from below, keep the fun in the game,
For pockets hold laughter, never quite the same!

Comfort in the Corners

In corners soft, I often find,
Lost treasures of a hilarious kind.
A sock that's lonely, a receipt so old,
They whisper stories, cheeky and bold.

A peanut from last year, not quite a snack,
Waving at me, like 'Hey, welcome back!'
Dust bunnies dance, a flurry of cheer,
In this little nook, life's light without fear.

A rogue button talks of fashion faux pas,
While lint offers gossip without a pause.
These corners keep secrets, mistakes from the past,
And comfort me, with laughter that lasts.

So here I sit, with crumbs and delight,
In the warmth of the corners, everything's right.
For who knew that fun could reside here at all?
In dusty old corners, I heed their small call.

Chasing Shadows of Thoughts

In the attic where shadows play,
Thoughts dance around in a silly ballet.
I chase them down with a twirl and a spin,
Guess what? They giggle as I let them in.

A thought of a sandwich, long since consumed,
Floats by my head, in a hat finely groomed.
It teases my hunger, then darts out of reach,
Making me ponder what lessons it'll teach.

Now why do they hide in the light?
These fleeting ideas, such a goofy sight!
A memory of socks, two left feet in the fray,
Zoom past my head in a comical way.

In the end, it's a race with my mind,
Chasing those shadows, oh so unconfined.
With humor in hand, I dance and I prance,
In shadows of thoughts, I just can't help but dance.

Revealed in the Stitchwork

In the quilt made from patches and rags,
Lies a story of mishaps, like lost old flags.
Each stitch holds a laughter, a tear, or a smile,
A war between fabric and threads without trial.

A patch of a cat with one eye that's winking,
Reminds me of times my old pal was thinking.
The colors collide, in a circus they play,
Bold reds and yellows, 'What a bright day!'

Behind every hem is a tale to be spun,
Of socks that went missing, but still have their fun.
A butterfly flying on thread made of gold,
Whispers to me grown-ups struggle with old.

So I cuddle my quilt, as laughter unfurls,
It wraps me in warmth, like the best kind of pearls.
In every seam, a joy rides the night,
A blanket of humor that feels just right.

Nostalgia's Hidden Chamber

Behind the old door, nostalgia does dwell,
Cracks in the wood, each has a tale to tell.
A rubber band sings of childhood's delight,
While crayons are plotting a colorful fight.

In this hidden chamber, I stumble upon,
Old toys that were cherished and now seem withdrawn.
A dust-covered teddy with one ear half gone,
Looks at me sideways, like 'Dude, carry on!'

The closet's alive with an audience grand,
Monsters of dirt in this unswept land.
Yet laughter and memories make all worth the mess,
In this charming old chamber, I'm surely blessed.

So let's take a trip to this wondrous bazaar,
In my mind's hidden chamber, we're never too far.
With giggles and glee, I return to each space,
In nostalgia's embrace, I find my own place.

Fabric of Forgotten Dreams

In the depths of my coat, dreams reside,
Buttons of laughter, pockets full of pride.
A sock of a story, mismatched in time,
Each thread a chuckle, each seam a rhyme.

Nibbled by mice or lost in the laundry,
Hopes tumble around like bits of pure folly.
Beneath the lint, wisdom waits in disguise,
Journeying with each mismatched surprise.

Forgotten dreams in denim and fleece,
Unfolding with giggles, granting release.
My pocket's a treasure, a whimsical space,
Where turnips and tickles both find their place.

So let's dig deep, no need for pretense,
In this bag of mischief, we'll laugh with sense.
For in every cranny, surprises await,
Dancing through fabric, life's silly fate.

Soft Echoes in the Weave

Softly tucked into the fabric of day,
Echoes of laughter find their own way.
Threads of absurdity, woven with cheer,
In pockets of stories, full of good beer.

A sandwich forgotten, still tastefully plush,
Whispers of past meals, in lunchtime rush.
A crumbled ticket from a show long gone,
Memory's laughter lingers on and on.

With crayons and doodles, a pocket might hold,
Tales of mischief that never grow old.
Spilling bright colors with a side of whim,
Artistry budding on a pocket's flim.

Even a crumpled receipt keeps a jest,
Of meals we devoured, a funny fest.
So let's dive into this tapestry seen,
For wisdom's a joke, made soft and clean.

Vestiges of Lived Experience

In pockets collection of odd little things,
A rogue paperclip and a button with wings.
Remnants of outings, escapades bold,
Each piece a tale that is waiting to be told.

A mint from last summer, now kinda stale,
With memories sprinkled, like breadcrumbs in trail.
A ticket from laughter, rolled tight with care,
Hints of the good times, softly laid bare.

Every bulge has a story, a giggle or blunder,
Flotsam and jetsam, life's bright silly wonder.
With pockets that rumble, and stories that sing,
Vibrations of joy from simple small things.

Let's hoot and let holler, share remnants we find,
For life's woven treasures are perfectly blind.
In the fabric of folly, we share what we feel,
With remains of our antics, each laugh is a steal.

Charm in the Unlikely

Worn pockets sagging, with charm and with grace,
Hold oddities wrapped in a colorful space.
A toothpick, a dandelion, hopes of a dance,
They laugh at us all with a playful romance.

A napkin with scribbles of dreams left to blend,
Whirlpool of nonsense where mismatches end.
Each item entrapped in fabric divine,
Bizarre little treasures that giggle in line.

A rubber band winks, as if in on the jest,
It stretches the truth, then it jiggles the rest.
With remnants of lunches and worn-out receipts,
This light-hearted journey is full of nice treats.

So here's to the chaos within all our seams,
In the land of the unlikely, we stitch up our dreams.
With each silly fragment that life gives a hug,
Declare your own joy in each soft, furry snug.

Threads of Memory Entwined

Within the seams of an old jacket,
Laughing ghosts play a game of whack-a-mole,
Each thread a story, a quirky fact,
A rogue button dances, it takes its toll.

Tightly tucked scraps hold secrets so bold,
A mismatched sock tells of adventures out there,
Stuck in the dryer, it spun tales untold,
While lint bunnies plot, with a mischievous glare.

A wallet's past echoes in crumpled bills,
Notes lost in chaos, half-eaten snacks,
Old receipts chatter of shopping thrills,
Each crumple a chuckle—a joy that never lacks.

In pockets wide, mischief makes its home,
Lost keys giggle at timeless disguise,
The stories they hide, like ripe fruit on a dome,
Turn mundane moments to comical highs.

Keeping Time in a Fold of Cloth

Inside a napkin, the clock seems to pause,
Tick-tock wrapped in crumbs of a sandwich feast,
Watches collide, in this fabric of flaws,
Time laughs and shrieks, unleashing the beast.

With spoons for hands, they dance through the years,
A teacup diary spills tales with glee,
A sugar cube holds the laughter, the tears,
When clocks become jesters, it's chaos, you see!

In collars of shirts, moments are trapped,
Calendars fold into tales of delight,
Unbuttons unearth memories untapped,
Every crease hides a party on a Wednesday night!

As pockets fold secrets and crinkled plans,
A rogue handkerchief waves to the crowd,
Time takes a bow, while laughter expands,
In this cloth kingdom, feel free to be loud!

Tales of Tattered Corners

In a corner of a page, history's a bit worn,
Crumpled whispers giggle—oh, such a glare,
Coffee stains tell of mornings reborn,
While each dog-eared hero spins stories to share.

A map with holes takes hilarious turns,
Lost socks lead to treasures in strange, wild lands,
Each tear reveals laughter and funny concerns,
A raccoon wearing glasses is tough to withstand.

Tattered borders are brimming with zest,
As toast crumbs narrate breakfast blunders,
Every frayed thread, a comedic quest,
In this circus of life, we dodge the thunders.

Let's gather the corners, bring laughter to light,
Each wrinkled relic sparks joy in a dance,
Forgotten giggles, two left feet take flight,
In this tattered tapestry, let whimsy prance!

The Quiet Connoisseur's Cache

Amongst the cloth, there's a stash so rare,
A folded fort hides marshmallows and dreams,
Sweet secrets simmer, with laughter to spare,
While jellybeans giggle in midnight schemes.

A thirst for comfort yields treasures galore,
Wrapped tightly with whimsy—what fun can arise?
Candy wrappers whisper to the coat's core,
As flavors collide, it's a feast in disguise.

In napkin folds, a gourmet delight,
Leftover pizza, an old-fashioned tryst,
With crumbs of the past, we savor the night,
For the quiet ones hold what the bold often missed.

This cache of laughter stirs up with a grin,
As memories tangle in humor's embrace,
With every soft fold, the joy creeps right in,
In the connoisseur's world, there's always a space!

Stories Hidden in Folds

In folds so deep, a mystery hides,
An old receipt, where humor resides.
A gum wrapper wrapped round a joke,
Whispers of laughter, from years bespoke.

Coins jingle like a merry tune,
Tales of a llama under a moon.
A lost sock, an adventurous fate,
Stitched in the seams, it can't be late.

Crumbs of cookies, crumbs of fun,
Leftovers from a picnic run.
In every crease, a tale to tell,
Of tiny triumphs, oh so swell.

So dive right in, take a peek inside,
Where oddities and laughter collide.
Each little treasure, a joyous find,
Reminds us to cherish, but not to bind.

Life's Trinkets Unearthed

A button here, a story in sight,
Of a dance-off gone awry at night.
A paperclip shaped like a heart,
Held jobs together but played its part.

A candy wrapper with a smiley face,
Whispers of sweets from a childhood place.
A crumpled note, a crush so bold,
"Will you go out? Please don't be cold!"

A tiny toy, half-buried in fluff,
A dinosaur who just wasn't tough.
Forgotten in pockets, ready to leap,
They bring back memories that make us weep.

So rummage around, don't be shy,
In those little details, let laughter fly.
Life's treasure trove, a quirky find,
With each trinket, joy intertwined.

Embracing the Everyday Marvels

A stray hairpin, holding time still,
Saved a bad hair day, quite a thrill.
A Tic Tac box, half full it lies,
"What's in there?" a surprise in disguise!

The lint's get together, a fluffy parade,
Reminds us it's fine to let dust invade.
With every pocket dive, secrets arise,
Funny old memories and goofy cries.

A wishbone from July's big feast,
Pulling for laughter, a joyful beast.
In everyday wonders, charm does lay,
Reminding us giggles are here to stay.

So let's embrace those bits we find,
Crafted with laughter, perfectly aligned.
For in these marvels, so richly spun,
Life's a comedy—join in the fun!

The Heirloom of Forgotten Dreams

An old key, rusty, a treasure of old,
Unlocking stories just waiting to unfold.
A whiff of perfume, sweetness and sly,
Echoes of dreams that flutter and fly.

A crinkle of paper, an artist's delight,
Scribbles of visions etched through the night.
Half-finished sketches, a giggle or two,
Hiding in pockets, old hopes anew.

A half-eaten sandwich, with tales to weave,
Of picnics forgotten, we hardly believe.
In each little fragment, a nugget of cheer,
Quirky legacies bring dreams near.

So treasure each item, no matter how small,
For wisdom is hidden in the oddest of all.
Inherit those giggles, those whispers of bliss,
For in laughter, we find what we truly miss.

Pocketful of Serendipity

Reaching inside for a little snack,
Found an old note, what a sweet whack!
'You owe me a dollar, my friend,' it read,
Guess I'll pay up when I'm rich instead.

A crumpled receipt, tales to unfold,
Of groceries bought, and stories old.
Yet here in my pocket, the best of the bunch,
Is a gumdrop I saved from my last lunch.

An odd mix of treasures, I proudly possess,
A paper clip, a lid, oh what a mess!
Yet when I dig deep, laughter's the prize,
Life's little quirks are the ultimate surprise.

So what if my pockets aren't neat and refined?
They're magnets for joy, the good kind!
Each time that I rummage, there's fun to ignite,
My pocket's a wonder, full of delight!

Charmed Life in a Small Space

In a pocket so tiny, adventure awaits,
A linty collection of bizarre dates.
A button, a penny, what stories they tell,
Each time that I search, I find a new spell.

A rubber band slingshots memories near,
Recalling the days of childhood cheer.
With gum stuck at the bottom, still sticky and bright,
My pocket's a vault of sheer pure delight.

Oh what joy blooms when I dig in deep,
For laughter and wisdom are what I keep.
In a charming small space, life's mysteries sing,
Like squirrels with acorns, I gather the bling!

So here's to the clutter, the chaos, the fun,
Who needs a big bag when I'm on the run?
A stick of old gum and a smile to embrace,
In my compact kingdom, I've found my place!

Gatherings of the Unseen

Inside my jeans, there's a world to explore,
Gatherings of wonders, who could ask for more?
A tiny lost napkin with doodles so grand,
The sketch of a dog with a ice cream stand.

A hairpin and bobby pins, all out of whack,
They twist and they turn, a jumbled track.
Yet when I do stumble upon this odd crew,
They're my pocket companions, oh how they grew!

Mysteries linger, like crumbs in a feast,
Collecting the stories, I'd never released.
A sprinkle of laughter, a dash of the strange,
These treasures of life, beautifully arranged.

Perks of the pockets, so silly and sly,
Like a magician's sleight, they tickle the eye.
Who needs a map when you've got your hand?
In the pocket's realm, joy is always planned!

Echoes in the Lining

What whispers come out from the depths of my clothes?
Echoes of laughter, as each pocket knows.
A rubber duck charm, how did it get there?
Traveling with me, from 1999 fair.

A forgotten candy, a relic of yore,
Exploring my pocket is never a bore.
Each slot holds a giggle, each crevice a cheer,
In the fabric of life, the fun's always near!

Like echoes of friends who have walked by my side,
Treasures of memories, they fill me with pride.
A lost little sock and a sprinkle of dust,
Pockets retain what the heart has discussed.

So here's to the fabric that dances with glee,
A pocket that whispers sweet secrets to me.
With every encounter, I jump and I sing,
For joy's in the lining, oh what a fling!

www.ingramcontent.com/pod-product-compliance
Lightning Source LLC
Chambersburg PA
CBHW060129230426
43661CB00003B/368